I0750278

FINISHING LINE PRESS
www.finishinglinepress.com

Impossible Bottle

poems by

Moriah Cohen

Finishing Line Press
Georgetown, Kentucky

"You are an aperture through which the universe is looking at and exploring itself."
—Alan Watts

"Bring in the bottled lightning, a clean tumbler, and a corkscrew."
—Charles Dickins

Impossible Bottle

For Nicky and Liam and Marc

ISBN 978-1-64662-574-1 First Edition

ACKNOWLEDGMENTS

Thank you to the editors of the following journals, in which some of the poems in this collection were first published:

Adroit Journal: "Snow Downgraded to Nuisance on the Narrow Street"
Hayden's Ferry Review: "Ontology" under the title "Ontology II"
Juked: "The Persistance of Memory"
Narrative Magazine: "Metempsychosis"
"Snow Downgraded to Nuisance on the Narrow Street" appeared also in the anthology *Best New Poets 2016* (University of Virginia Press in cooperation with *Meridian*).

Publisher: Leah Huete de Maines
Editor: Christen Kincaid
Cover Art and Design: Jessica Cohen
Author Photo: Seth Pullum

Order online: www.finishinglinepress.com
also available on amazon.com

Author inquiries and mail orders:
Finishing Line Press
PO Box 1626
Georgetown, Kentucky 40324
USA

Table of Contents

ONTOLOGY

In a picture bisected by a collision of sky
and plateau, an artist has photographed herself

photographing her own deflagrated body.
First thought: how Jungian. How binary

to sequence life in ones and zeros, instead of a schema
where any choice means infinite versions of us

never breathe. Same concept: at a certain age,
our brains prune synapses we don't use,

a weeding of the mind that makes learning
language clamorous, but allows me to remember

it was Jung too who intimated dreaming
as a type of translation, and to wonder then

what it says that last night I hewed myself
into splinters, woke begging him to tell

which me shivered against him in the dark.

ON MY BIRTHDAY, A WOMAN CROSSES A HIGHWAY IN THE RAIN

leaving pretense in the road like a cat

I just hit with my car. *It's not your fault,*
I say, unbuckling my belt, shutting

a door behind me. Two a.m., back streets
distended with suffering, but I can't

remember the closet where I left the umbrella.
Instead, I am thinking of the boy

in that commercial who's so hungry,
his eyes lick me clean.

I've tried to tell the cashier that lately a fog
leans over me, but the cashier only sees

down my shirt, like he's supposed to reach
inside and tear out the Wendigo heart

he recognizes as his own, how it stirs
in the stillness after nesting dolls break,

how it fights its way from my chest.

POEM OF REPLYS TO MY INBOX AFTER A BREAK-UP

12.46 is too much for insurance
when the neighbor's deliveries sprout
sidewalk and crack leaves.

The railing of the kids' bed
rises to the ceiling like prayer or possession,
a TV crashing against a wall
and spilling its guts.

Always wanted to try
boxing though I don't have
the nose for it.

The redolence of pine
climbing through my window
was all it took to secure a refund
for collapsible
trekking poles whose instinct
I should have known
would be to collapse at the first sign
of a rock.

If survival is a question
of uniform—

If magpieing the pink slough
of a backpack, stuffing
two sleeping bags and a hammock
next to the door
were enough to feel
self-determined—

I untuck the tips of my glasses
from behind my ears,
and high school girls catching
breath in the building's shade
look sun-dusted, untender
like pockets setting below
the fingered rim of shorts
as they laugh with the gravity
of a planet.

I thought I could begin again:
I paid rent and pulled long
slivers of blond from my mouth
in half-lit alleys.

I hated the burnt dumpster
smell and how he said
he couldn't help but look
at high school girls jogging
then feel guilty for looking.

It was what I wanted to mourn
but couldn't find
words for.

Instead, I picked at branches.
Every one of three infested
with sacks of silk and needle
hanging from boughs,
bristling brown, and hollowing
the bodies that housed them.

I THINK OF THE YEAR I TRIED TO RID THE HOUSE OF LADY BUGS

the house
like a ceramic moose ear
accepting loose change and keys and buttons;

hundreds of ladybugs choking living room
window-frames, clambering over each other,
and flinging small hefts into glass.

They sensed by moonglow, November
pinching at the interstices freedom.

Logs cracked in the fireplace.

A young wife, I was not restless
exactly.
Inexactly,
the instinct to stopper a hole
flickered stoically in front of me, winged and scarlet,

and I midwifed
a self to stand next to the girl
thawing near the flames.

It squirmed
into the world, and my job was to coax it
from the girl's mouth; the most terrible
and holy of openings
thrashing.

I was lying when I said I tried to rid the house of ladybugs.
I bundled myself in them
as if they were a blanket.

In the morning, they were all dead,
and I vacuumed tiny corpses from the floor
and the window ledge, and sometimes,
from the corduroy couch.

But by evening, they returned,
the accumulation of Rorschach wings,

carving in the window
the trough of a wave, of a stammering sky.

UPON LEARNING DUTCH TEARS CAN BE BROKEN ONLY BY CHIPPING THE TAIL

1

Whistles skitter toward a skein of cherry blossoms
so terminal my shoulder aches.

Across town, blackbirds unthread straw
from planters, harvest wrappers from garbages,
repurpose floss.

Their dead babies appear on the car
shortly after, stiffened bodies the size
of pendants only battered into grotesque
facsimiles of life—a beak
cocked at an impossible angle,
a gnarl of feathers ropy, soiled.

We don't notice the dead at first.
But the living fly down from unfinished
nests to shit on the car next to the body.

Mourning ritual or lesson, we wonder,
as birds line eaves, and we run
out of milk.

Blusters of wings blow petals skittish.
One storm begets another, both swooning.

The sun perches adrift over the cherry
blossom tree, and M shovels the newest
dead into a vase, before slipping into the garage
to weld us a future.

I watch petals descend in pink wisps.

Sparks snap in the garage; an arc of electricity
looking for somewhere to jump,
finds only a seam of metal.

I dig a grave for the bird larger
than the hole inside me.

A veil falls, plume after petal, as I dig,
binds surfaces until the yard wears
the corrugated shimmer of a tin roof
too blinding to gaze into.

2

Call it thermal—blackbirds knowing
when to mate, to move on.

My sudden desire to be condensed
then strained until I'm a jingle of seeds.

In the garden, I keep finding shells
the shape of a bullet or a planet
cracked open.

I make of their rooms
tiny mutinies; impress a floret between
the pages of Decartes' *Meditations*,
splatter paint on a crosshatched
husk and tac it to a wall.

The facts as best I see them:
More of my eggs are flailing,
mossy now than not.

More teeth notched with worry.

In the mirror, I crook my bottom lip
like it's being dragged offstage after flopping
a joke and swear
I've never seen the back left molar
stripped black before—it's painful to touch.

Let's be honest: a hushed *fuck*,
a crumpled wrapper bearing the cartoon image
of a shirtless man are all it takes to riot
my womb an army.

I slink into the garage where M is fabricating

a mold of a furnace for his studio.

The air is so hot it decants metallic
blue feathers, the consistency of habit,
instinct too bleary to decipher.

There is nothing that is not in process.

Darkness pools where M's shirt
clutches his body.

Later, we will find sweat huddled,
clinging to windows, but now, noonday sirens
rising, we bear so much thirst.

3

We were waiting, just waiting,
which is to say, I was scrubbing days
like toilets.

On my knees, collecting rust, grime
from corners, ceiling fans.

It's true what we think we possess
finds ways to allude us:

wind knocking a streetlamp dark,
a stone kicked loose from the retaining wall
of our understanding.

All hours, sirens screamed out
from the volunteer rescue squad, dusk
fanned across a chopping block.

I doused olives in rosemary,
faint and sharp as promises, skinned
and seared tuna, splashed another glass
half-full of Nebbiolo.

Then, the squirrel lady—every morning

scattering peanuts from
her porch and calling squirrels

to revelation—started yelling from inside
her porch's white pillars, *God help him,*
he can't breathe.

We didn't think anyone else lived there,
until the ambulance pulled up and the cops,
and after watching red and blue lights
spill down the dark street, a silhouette
strapped to a stretcher,

we shut the blinds, returned to our show
out of modesty or boredom or fear.

4

Let's be honest:
flame broiled black char
on the bottom of the sheetpan.

Lines of shoppers wearing
bandanas and N95s snaked
three blocks from the Trader Joes.

I could never tell the difference
between a blackbird and a back porch,
but I know if I close my eyes,
slump my body—

Sometimes, I wonder if conditional
reality is a defect
simmering on a back burner,

like somehow, I'm not walking home,
arms leaden with groceries, but falling
really far from some minor height.

Near the park, police string caution tape,
whoop sirens to flicker kids from the riverwalk.

When Prince Rupert
smuggled his glass tears to England
in 1660, he did it as a magic trick
to convince that a center could,
in fact, hold.

For every branch taken, a nest
appears in its place.

For every shadow knocking around
inside us an equivalent
inexhaustible, shattering light.

I COULD NOT TELL HIM

My dog whines outside the door of my room.

He is all ears, my little pepper, when brie
and shrimp tendrils and mushrooms come out
on chipped lighthouse plates, and his ears
perch like the ears of bats, wide upon his head.

Still fermenting, beer swills the insides
of our mugs molasses.

I trim stems of chrysanthemum,
then puncture each one on the spiny
frog at the center of a Japanese vase.

M only buys me dead things,
so I cannot kill them.

Their smell is sweet like *lacuna*, a word
I keep for myself to describe
intervals between the colors of a grackle
that barks through my body.

He is large and clean. The breeze
rustles his stoic feathers on the green roof,
though his eyes squint out of many paintings.

His eyes are still lives.

His eyes are streets I scuff down
until I do not remember names for the manners
that housed me.

Equidistant birch damming black river,
scaffolded towers of the refinery beyond the highway
juicing smoky moonlight
cannot be consoled by the bite of his talons.

In our mugs, sugar swoons
frothy and blackstrap. To distill is to replace
sweetness with something fugitive.

REMOVE YOUR SANDALS FROM YOUR FEET

A fleet of coxed-fours pulls
daybreak downriver, lanterns
nodding in the still-dark
run of each stroke whose presence
beneath the bridge means
I am late for work.
Most mornings, I skirt
bucket seats abandoned on shoulders,
the way the beltway
skirts town as if waiting for it
to wash on shore like all the other
gutted things that find the bank.
I'm not sure why
when adjusting the mirror
today or shifting down to second gear
to match the traffic's
undertow, I imagine
the missing plane from the news,
its passengers both
alive and dead somewhere
in the unknowable expanse of silence
that for Schrödinger was a box
with a cat. And for Moses
a turning.
And if later, I turn
toward the turbine of M's body,
it is more a taste for fluency
than the body itself
which strokes a vast
darkness. A taste for fluency
we enter, bodies ashudder,
because in that moment,
we are drowning,
we are never found.

IMPOSSIBLE BOTTLE

I crawl behind a dark curtain
into a small room—

the ceiling is a sky of equidistant
lightbulbs so dim
they barely fill themselves.

When the show starts,
lights blink a pattern
suggestive of a hawk
swooping between viewer and stars.

The show starts with perception
and ends in prophecy.

Both times I gave birth
I hovered above myself,
steering a full-rigged
ship through a dark screen.

And when what the doctor
tore out of me was a clot
of barbed wire, I lifted it
to my chest with arms
I borrowed from the sea.

WHY THE ARK HAD NO NAME

Because it was christened with wine.

Because pockets of marsh
scarfed our feet plum and bone before
lapping into echo.

Because no bottle would shatter against that stern.

Because a seam tore open, and our friends
slipped inside.

Because though we felt it in our ankles,
the knots of our fingers, we could not admit
we were redeemable.

Because masks paraded down canals
we never travelled.

Because if shore is a thing of courage, it espouses
faith: reeds the size of temple walls towered
for want of light, a garbled sill we toed for in the muck.

Because despite customer lines glutting
checkouts, aisles had already been ransacked
of toilet paper, pasta, frozens, soap.

Because it took five days for the sea to belch
a drowned body.

Because night is just another word for sea.

Because the president's hair declared
the country exceptional, and the woman behind
his speech bobbed her head like a buoy.

Because when M pawed his way to bed,
we were water inside of water.

Because they padlocked schools,
warned us to stay inside.

Because without planks to thrust against,
the sea did not know itself.

Because rain hammered a gully inside me.

Because animals came like a storm
in the billow of my womb.

Because M and the boys and I tore at arugula
and beetroot and cabbage.

Because I sucked leaf after fleshly leaf
from the artichoke, and the leaves kept coming.

Because there was no heart at its center.

Because the boys played that game
where they machinegun each other
in the eye of a storm.

Because M kept welding a future in his shop.

Because I missed my mother, and what kind of father.

Because how does one say my fear is an ocean?

Because the stench of instinct
splintered wood I was afraid to run
my fingers across.

Because we drew lots to thatch
wounds, to bucket shit we heaved starboard.

Because ants floated in my coffee like lost stars.

REREADING PLATH, I THINK OF THE OLD BRAG AS AN ATTEMPT TO TWEEZE DIVINITY FROM THE TROUGH OF A HEARTBEAT

Grab my mask and drive out to the landscape
place to pick up with M.

Last full sun, before forecasts
bleed a week of wolves.

I'm half lash, half lector, leather
crowding my thighs in the bucket

of a Jeep, falsetto hammering
wings inside my throat:

I want to be your mother
and your sister, too.

M keeps skidding the truck
toward pillars three quarters

up a hill-face we never make,
gravel tossing behind us

like laughter, the pillars'
thin scrolls ahead of us unraveling

a porch front—what might
be called religion

if we wiped our feet there.
Lately, I think it is

someone else churning
my fingers into the earth's

soft belly as the moon
hunches darkly as a jailor.

What womb howls for M to fill it
with the shape of a name?

Reaching toward him
is like reaching for a town

I don't remember I know
until our tires glint

down a turn, and I can direct
the slope of tin roofs

flicking the valley,
chimneys calibrating tiny

puffs that grip the air.

GALATEA SPEAKS

Yes, you knew me
even before you puffed
small breaths
into my mouth, and I glowed
a swirling bubble which you pulled
like taffy.

All I knew was flame,
though I couldn't cull it—

the way your hands
bloated, and the steel pipe
swelled the eddies of your fingers
until you had no name.

You whispered a window
I gazed out of.

I was the window whose louvered
shutters you glued to the siding.

At night, maple silhouettes
tilted their hewn ears
toward the patter of water.

We waited for roots to come.

When you drew me a bath,
it was to cool the tremors
bruising my chest.

It was to beg the trees
break open the walls.

THE PERSISTENCE OF MEMORY

For Gala Dalí

who raged water electricity and heat when the shack had none

who fried her pet rabbit and fucked like an electric eel

who wore a cathedral on her head

whose head was a throne towering over gables
and domes of the Mediterranean and sometimes a head of snakes

who bartered bills and paid for bruised fruit

whose second husband named her a tree of names
that grew no fruit
only long stalks dangling from branches

who ten years his senior squeezed herself
into his mouth so she could inhabit his body

who walked naked and ate naked and swam naked
and whose nipples were the needles of a compass
pointing always toward the dirt but also out to sea

who night after night dreamt only of the sea and the surf
curving around her like a hook

who was born from the barrel of a horse

who was born outside a womb to many fathers

whose bones grew conical like the horns of a rhinoceros
which she pulled painful from her mouth like an armory
of bayonets, until she had no bones and her mouth refused to close

who fucked Paul Élutard and Max Ernest and Jeff Fenholt and their lovers

who fucked body shivering white clover in the breeze

who shivering climbed a staircase of vertebrae
and disassembled the earth into spheres

who committed herself to antiseptic rooms that her lovers
wandered in their nightmares and that she rearranged when the moon
slivered over the roof until the lovers were lost in darkness

who saw Jesus crucified at Port Lligat in darkness and the sea was whistling

who bound to a tree bled roses from her uterus
as a shadow cast over her and a parenthesis closed

THE THING INSIDE ME THAT CONSUMES EVERYTHING

The dead bird next to the pepper plant is sprouting maggots from its chest.

It's my fault I didn't shovel it into the trash when I could;
pay the water bill; sign Devin up for that class where they art plastics
China no longer takes.

I shop around.

An island of trash sleeps off its bender.

Three days expired, milk doesn't clump into coffee, but it's close.

Tomorrow is the day
whirring next to the window, east-bound the reckoning.

Maggots writhe through the bird's chest like strings unseaming a toy.

Larvae of a string-puller says: you did not do enough with your life, so I undo you; says: the revolution leaves nothing but skulls and plastic feet.

It's all televised:
the bird's wings splayed like hurricane and the stench crowning.

It's still better than watching presidential hopefuls on the news.

No trash is an island, one headline claims, and I swear, in the background, the maggots are ripping themselves into smaller maggots.

On days when I cannot find words, Devin and I wander the labyrinth of a Target.

Pushing a red cart, I hunt for clearance toys to camouflage us, and wonder whether there is a word long enough to string a life on.

At home, when Devin falls asleep, I slurp wings and drink Two Buck Chuck from a sugar bowl which maggots' do not find uncouth.

I get drunk and see how long it takes to have the pipes repossessed.

What's left is thriving.

During commercials, I count miracles backwards toward Genesis.

My parents named me after the mountain where Abraham intended to sacrifice his child.

Each miracle is a keeled sternum, I think.

I gnaw each one to the gristle.

SNOW DOWNGRADED TO NUISANCE ON THE NARROW STREET

Houses wake with light by the mug-full—
parades of underarmor and boots; cars
backfire then shimmy to a start.

The second time
we're born they say will be of fire.

The third of snow.

But coaxing the boy's
arms through his sleeves, the woman knows
this time he was born an elephant which is
to say he is an obelisk and a rope.

Just last night, she woke to the radio
looping a station's jingle followed by
militants dragging a foreign city by its
spindly legs.

She turned on the lamp. Or she didn't.

She swaddled her little elephant in wet
darkness that branched like pines
that ring the house.

These hours fray at the tips,
peal or tip-toe, want what they want, if only bodies
to knead the swollen mouth, massage
from the pain a shape as she coaxes them
through sleep.

Dalí's joke: the animal does not know
where it ends nor begins.

And there is something swanlike about that,
isn't there? A beauty that hurts so bad
in its understanding of its own loneliness.

Once, she saw a cygnet spill across the confusion
of a white lake.

At water's center rested an island.
On the island, black trunks blanching at the tips.

THE PINES

After Leadbelly

On the wrong side
of a back door,
pines unfold limbs, reedy and swaying.

A clot of leaves, fur
swept from living room corners
shake in one tree's raw branches
where a crow foraged a nest.

Forget what we shed:
a down graveyard the dog
chewed from the comforter;
callouses carved

from your palm to test
the knife's edge;
a stronghold dismantled stone
by stone from around
the outpost of the self.

No one tells you
that woods sleepwalk,

that when you lift
your head from the pillow
of your sleeve, you will not
have a name to call.

The world is not,
I am convinced, for us,
though we keen at its longing.

Admit it, you know
where I slept—where nettles sheet
the ground, and the crow,
barking, peels his feathers.

In the darkness,
he is a single eye
picking at the dirt.

I DID NOT SHOW YOU HOW I THREW DOWN

my gloves after a life was pulled out of me kicking.

I smashed cameras and wedded myself
to a silence that ministered over me.

The silence was not for you.

You were what filled it.

What I swished around my mouth,
until I remembered to breathe.

What I kept feeding with faith it would speak.

I THINK OF PROMETHEUS AND WONDER IF ANY PARCEL OF MY BODY IS EVEN WORTH PUNISHMENT FOR SOME CONSIDERABLE DEED

Half-choking on the rancor of a Victorian collar, I am happy my ex bears a life he hasn't yet figured the rules to.

Devin trips up the sidewalk in front of my ex and I who play catchup, trading a live-in girlfriend for a job, a job for a philosophy.

From some planet, Earth is moving retrograde, and Devin is not a boy in a skeleton costume, but a boy in the costume of a man costumed in mischief, an avatar harvesting firearms, hunkering down supplies in the shrinking eye of a hurricane, where winter is the last survivor, and the sky a swirling purple marble.

Parents are trailing Bourbon and pulling kegs on RadioFlyers.

Parents at the end of the night drag their Adirondack chairs to the mouths of a few yards, outdoor fireplaces glowing cycloptic.

At the far end of a dream, I slice a part down the center of my hair, sink a guthook into a lamb's sternum. A scale squeals and bobs like the one in the vegetable aisle onto which I might place a lettuce, then tabulate the head's cost.

Depending whom I ask, in carving organs from an animal's carcass, ritual wanders either toward or away from prayer.

I cup my ear against ground.

I lick my finger then hold it up to locate a gusting inside me.

In old myths, duality meant gods entering women as swans, meant women welded at the back tearing themselves from a womb, only the further they tore from each other, the more the sticky sheath between them resembled throbbing wings.

New myths are less ambitious, beg only survival.

Each day is a new step.

Today, I mount layers of clothes on top of each other to keep Devin and I warm, to keep from getting sick.

My promises are translucent—it will be okay, I say, squirreling food, caching change in a pillowcase at the top of the closet next to a one-hitter that looks like a gutted hog.

SOMEDAYS PARENTING BE LIKE:

my right sandal sucked into a flash flood
and rerouted to the sewer grate on my way to the laundry mat.

A thick curtain of rain
marches forward. It's like at the theater,
the curtain. It's like Macbeth, and a forest

marching rogue branches, an army stroked
bark and green, but with no audience to tell me
it's over. No crook to lure me

away from gesture and into my solitude.
I shit bouncing Rich on my lap. A girl with whom
I graduated from college composes

articles on the misogyny of monsters which I read
while Rich roots at my nipple.
My breasts lumber with milk.

Some days it is like falling from midway
across a limb. How Rich screams crook
and lure at three a.m., and I sit up and stroke

his straw hair while he tries to articulate darkness.
How the theater of our bodies marches
imperceptibly forward, and then three-pronged

and hissing, a man is telling me, I want to live
with my father. So I ask him, *What*
father? And *Isn't this life enough for you?*

But, we are all forests, even Rich twisting ivy
from the trellis and weeding green buds
that crack the steps.

While Rich sleeps, I reach into his chest
and remove the bone around which his cells
adhered and became a body. It is like reaching

into a past that never materialized. It is like
my body has done this thing countless times,

though I can't remember, and Rich is crying

so loud and I am crying so loud that the crying
is electric. And then Rich goes slack and crawls
around the floor, until his legs are strong enough

to carry him again. Until tiny white moths
alight from the grass as he takes a step.

WHEN YOU'RE LOST AND ALL ALONE THERE AIN'T NO WORD BUT LONELY

I had this dream visiting my aunt's in Falmouth.
She was living alone then, after four
marriages to three husbands, a salt's
throw from the beach.

The neighborhood had no sidewalks,
but most days we walked a few bends
along a shoulder, parading single file,
half-in, half-out of pitch
and scrub oak brush grating at our calves,
grinding shrift into asphalt.

In the dream, I peered down on a cul-de-sac,
nailed wood to the casement windows
of my aunt's house, as men, nighted
in balaklava, tried to force their way in.

Like most dreams, this one exhaled
the syrupy air of the predetermined,
so when a man shattered the glass between broken
planks dangling on the door, I swallowed
my pulse, but was not surprised, and reached
beneath the couch for hedge clippers
I found hidden there the next morning,
while my aunt burnt French Toast.

I want to say the house my aunt lived in
was ranch-style, one story.
Though maybe I mistake the house
in my mind for the one in which all women
dwell—humble, bloody.

Years later, I lived in a foreign place,
and every night my husband travelled
for work, I dragged our mattress
to my sons' room and buried it in their green
shag carpet, a domestic
thrift we meant to weed, but never did.

Look at the knife dreaming beneath

my pillow—the only sleep. Look at how
a woman becomes a corn field, all goose-
flesh and ear and small husks peeling.

Do you understand?

I keep thinking of this song
strangers used sing to me when I was young
in which mercy is the wind
uprooting a house—as if I should
be that mercy.

The song goes, *When you're lost*
and all alone, there ain't no word but lonely.

But at night, I uncover other words
for sticky-sweet palms lingering for harvest,
for sons sidling to sleep, for voices
hardening into cords of wood.

METEMPSYCHOSIS

For weeks I've shared this balcony with coffee
and book, some illegible notion
steaming from the street below
of you.
Elsewhere,
perhaps here too, regimes stagger,
a congress ends. What is there to say
about the clatter of people passing that cannot be,
just as easily, swallowed in silence?
Last night I dreamt two deserts and knew one
was the gulf opening inside me,
the other a postcard misaddressed:
come home.
When I think back, it must have been
someone else who hitched
across the Sangre de Cristos with you,
snaked into barbed-wire
graveyards to lace wooden crosses with fireweed.
Not me.
I've never been a high-road
girl even when it was strung with pueblos.
Peaks so old, at dusk, a pyretic
voice coughs up your name with the dust.
What was it Georgia O'Keeffe said about vast
and empty and untouchable beauty
knowing no kindness?
On the front of the postcard:
aria of chile, claret cups.
In my dream, the man feeding me
agave has no face, but I know it is you, crouched
in this landscape we've sculpted,
spade and mattock, between us—
a routine to bury ourselves in.
In the desert there is a saying: it is better
to have a sharp knife than a sharp memory.
Still, late, I remember bleached bones,
smoke from the controlled burn
climbing the back of Truchas as you guided
my hand over nopalitos, teaching me
to peel them without upsetting the spines.

WHEN WE CANNOT ANYMORE TAKE

fecund damp curling
blossoms on the other side
of spring, and M's roommate
has sculpted the last rolls
of toilet paper into two runny
eyes, clipped an empty
between seat and closed
lid so the toilet looks
like it's smoking
a blunt, M and I ride
along a strip of sand that feeds
the ocean small rivulets.
In the copse behind low tide,
poison ivy clambers up
concrete slabs that rise
from the dunes; so tightly
cups the warbling
yellow of crumbling
military bunkers, it cleaves
the foundation into paths.
Don't tell me what
I cannot touch.
What the world claims
when it is through
laughing, it claims like M's
fingers, teasing knots
from my hair. The roughness
of my knuckles
scrapes a thousand tiny
guillotines. Bunker doors
screech to be rattled
open—no
crouching dark could make me
grasp for this world
any less.

NOTES

The book's epigraphs are from Alan Watt's lecture "On Seeing Oneself in the Correct Way," later printed in *Still the Mind: An Introduction to Meditation* and from Charles Dicken's novel, *Nicholas Nickleby.*

"Ontology" was informed by a series of photographs by Sabrina Occhipinti.

"On my Birthday, A Woman Crosses a Highway in the Rain" contains a reference to a commercial for the Christian Children's Fund.

"Upon Learning Dutch Tears can be Broken Only by Chipping the Tail" refers to a glass tear characterized by high residual internal stresses. If hit on the bulbous end, a Dutch Tear can withstand a blow from a hammer; however, if the tail is even slightly shaken, the tear will explosively shatter. The poem also nods to William Butler Yeats' "The Second Coming." It is informed by a quote attributed to The Mother in *Questions and Answers 1950-1951*, a transcript of conversations based on Sri Aurobindo's book *The Mother*: "You carry in yourself all the obstacles necessary to make your realization perfect. Always you will see that within you the shadow and the light are equal .... If you discover a very black hole, a thick shadow, be sure there is somewhere in you a great light. It is up to you to know how to use the one to realize the other."

"Remove your Sandals from your Feet" refers to Exodus 3:5 of the *New American Standard Bible* in which God says to Moses, "Remove your sandals from your feet, for the place on which you are standing is holy ground." The poem references a stretch of New Jersey Route 20 that runs adjacent to the Passaic River, as well as Malaysian Airlines Flight 370, which disappeared on March 8, 2014.

"Impossible Bottle" was informed by Jim Campbell's "Tilted Plane" which appeared at the Whitney Museum of American Art from September 28, 2018 to April 14, 2019 in the exhibit *Programmed: Rules, Codes, and Choreographies in Art 1965-2018.*

"Why the Ark had no Name" refers to Genesis 6 and Genesis 7 of the *New American Standard Bible.* It contains to a reference to *Fortnite*, a videogame by Epic Games.

"Reading Plath I Think of the Old Brag as an Attempt to Tweeze Divinity from the Trough of a Heartbeat" refers to a quote from Sylvia Plath's The Bell Jar: "I took a deep breath and listened to the old brag of my heart: I am, I am, I am." It quotes a line from Prince's "I Wanna be your Lover."

"The Persistence of Memory" was informed by the permanent collection at the Salvador Dalí Museum in Saint Petersburg, Florida, as well as by the exhibit *Dalí Revealed: Candid Moments from the Artist's Life* which appeared at the Salvador Dalí Museum from May 19, 2015 through December 3, 1017.

"The Thing Inside me that Consumes Everything" contains a reference to the Great Pacific Garbage Patch and a riff on a sentence from John Donne's "Meditation XVII," "No man is an island entire of itself." "Two-Buck Chuck" is a nickname for Charles Shaw wine.

"Snow Downgraded to Nuisance on the Narrow Street" contains references to Salvador Dalí's 1937 painting "Swans Reflecting Elephants" and his 1948 painting "Elephants."

"In the Pines" takes its title from an American folksong of the same name. The song's authorship is unknown, but it was sung by Lead Belly in one of its earliest recordings.

"I Think of Prometheus and Wonder if Any Parcel of my Body is even Worth Punishment for Some Considerable Deed" contains to a reference to *Fortnite*, a videogame by Epic Games.

"When You are Lost and All Alone There Ain't No Word but Lonely" takes its title from "They Call the Wind Maria," a song whose lyrics were written by Alan J. Lerner for the 1951 Broadway Musical *Painted Wagon*.

In "Metempsychosis," the referenced Georgia O' Keeffe's quote (1943) discusses animal skulls she collected in the New Mexico desert: "The bones seem to cut sharply to the center of something that is keenly alive on the desert even though it is vast and empty and untouchable—and knows no kindness with all its beauty."

"When we Cannot Anymore Take" contains a reference to Fort Hancock, a former United States Army Fort in Sandy Hook, New Jersey.

Additional Acknowledgments

Thanks to Finishing Line Press for opportunity and for the pride with which you produce other people's visions.

Thank you, James Hoch, for warning me I had vision.

Thanks to Matthew Lippman under whose tutelage many of these poems found form.

Thanks to Rachel Hadas and Rigoberto González and my other professors at Rutgers-Newark's MFA program whose advice and criticism and support prodded me forward, and for the program scholarship which allowed me, as a young, single mother, to afford graduate school.

Thanks to my workshopping cohort Jared Beloff and Rachael Combe and Troy Wennet for being critical of my words, but courteous with your own, and to Poets House for uniting us.

Thanks to my sister-in-law Jessica Cohen for creating the art for the book cover and to my less official sister-in-law Ariella Planas for helping with author photographs.

Love and indebtedness to my parents and my brother for unconditionally supporting me, and to the friends and family, including my ex-husband, Ian Miller, who have been kind enough to keep me.

To Nicky and Liam, for altering the course of my life irreconcilably and for putting your dishes in the sink.

To Marc, my first reader, my most honest editor, my dearest friend—every day you inspire.

www.ingramcontent.com/pod-product-compliance
Lightning Source LLC
LaVergne TN
LVHW051022080826
845145LV00009B/2756

* 9 7 8 1 6 4 6 6 2 5 7 4 1 *